The Language of
LABS

The Language of
LABS

■ WILLOW CREEK PRESS®

Published by Willow Creek Press, Inc.
P.O. Box 147, Minocqua, Wisconsin 54548

Photo Credits:

p2-3 © J. A. Kraulis/Masterfile; p5 © Faith A. Uridel/www.kimballstock.com; p7 © Lynn M. Stone/www.kimballstock.com; p8 © Gerard Lacz/age fotostock; p11 © Ron Kimball/www.kimballstock.com; p12 © Sam Allen/www.kimballstock.com; p16 © Denver Bryan/www.kimballstock.com; p19 © Juniors Bildarchiv/age fotostock; p20 © Toronto Star/age fotostock; p23 © Juniors Bildarchiv/age fotostock; p24 © Klein-Hubert/www.kimballstock.com; p27 © Denver Bryan/www.kimballstock.com; p28 © Juniors Bildarchiv/age fotostock; p31 © Ron Kimball/www.kimballstock.com; p32 © Denver Bryan/www.kimballstock.com; p35 © Denver Bryan/www.kimballstock.com; p36 © Reneé Stockdale/www.kimballstock.com; p39 © Winter-Churchill/www.kimballstock.com; p40 © Juniors Bildarchiv/age fotostock; p43 © Ron Kimball/www.kimballstock.com; p44 © Labat-Rouquette/www.kimballstock.com; p47 © Paul Wright/Masterfile; p48 © Juniors Bildarchiv/age fotostock; p51 © Justin Paget/age fotostock; p52 © Juniors Bildarchiv/age fotostock; p55 © Denver Bryan/www.kimballstock.com; p56 © Denver Bryan/www.kimballstock.com; p59 © PICANI/age fotostock; p64 © John Lund/www.kimballstock.com; p67 © Juniors Bildarchiv/age fotostock; p68 © Juniors Bildarchiv/age fotostock; p71 © Gary Randall/www.kimballstock.com; p72 © PICANI/age fotostock; p75 © Denver Bryan/www.kimballstock.com; p76 © Juniors Bildarchiv/age fotostock; p79 © Denver Bryan/www.kimballstock.com; p80 © Juniors Bildarchiv/age fotostock; p83 © Ron Kimball/www.kimballstock.com; p84 © ARCO/H Frei/age fotostock; p87 © Denver Bryan/www.kimballstock.com; p88 © Juniors Bildarchiv/age fotostock; p91 © Mike Randolph/Masterfile; p92 © Daniela Hofer/age fotostock; p95 © Minden Pictures/age fotostock; p96 © Labat-Rouquette/www.kimballstock.com

Design: Donnie Rubo
Printed in China

The only valid excuse for not exercising is paralysis.

—*Moira Nordholt*

ATHLETICISM

If you cannot do great things, do small things in a great way.

—*Napoleon Hill*

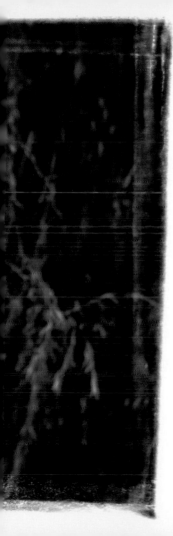

Fortune befriends the bold.

—John Dryden

BRAVERY

Courage is resistance to fear, mastery of fear—
not absence of fear. Except a creature be part
coward it is not a compliment to say it is brave.

—Mark Twain

Keep your spirits up. Good things will come
to you and you will come to good things.

—*Glorie Abelhas*

CHEERFULNESS

Wherever you go, no matter what the weather,
always bring your own sunshine.

—*Anthony J. D'Angelo*

Contentment is natural wealth,
luxury is artificial poverty.

—*Socrates*

CONTENTMENT

My riches consist not in the extent of my
possessions, but in the fewness of my wants.

—*J. Brotherton*

Faithfulness and sincerity are the highest things.

—*Confucius*

DEVOTION

Faithfulness lives where love is stronger than instinct.

—*Paul Carvel*

I arise full of eagerness and energy, knowing well
what achievement lies ahead of me.

—Zane Grey

ENTHUSIASM

Enthusiasm is the sparkle in your eyes, the swing in your
gait… the irresistible surge of will and energy.

—Henry Ford

Let us not pray to be sheltered from dangers,
but to be fearless when facing them.
—*Rabindranath Tagore*

FEARLESS

To be fearless yet free from hate is a state
of being to which we should all strive
—*Unknown*

What is courageous in one setting
can be foolhardy in another.
–Unknown

FOOLHARDY

Few things are brought to a successful
issue by impetuous desire, but most
by calm and prudent forethought.
—Thucydides

Love thy neighbor, and if it requires that you bend your understanding of the truth, the Truth will understand.

—*Robert Brault*

FRIENDLY

I always prefer to believe the best of everybody. It saves so much trouble.

—*Rudyard Kipling*

This life is not for complaint, but for satisfaction.
—*Henry David Thoreau*

FULFILLMENT

Occasionally in life there are those moments of unutterable fulfillment which cannot be completely explained by those symbols called words. Their meanings can only be articulated by the inaudible language of the heart.
—*Martin Luther King, Jr.*

We are furtively drawn to temptation by its furtive gaze.

—*Unknown*

FURTIVE

In everyone there is an air of incorrigible innocence,
which seems to conceal a diabolical cunning.

—*A.E. Housman*

Only the weak are cruel. Gentleness can
only be expected from the strong.
—*Leo F. Buscaglia*

GENTLENESS

There never was any heart truly great and generous,
that was not also tender and compassionate.
—*Robert Frost*

Happiness is not a matter of intensity but of
balance, order, rhythm and harmony.
—*Thomas Merton*

HARMONY

Just because man no longer understands his place in
the universe, don't let him assume all God's creatures
have become equally confused and trivial.
—*Bill Tarrant*

In about the same degree as you are helpful, you will be happy.

—Karl Reiland

HELPFUL

Being good is commendable, but only when
it is combined with doing good is it useful.

—Unknown

I can't think of any sorrow in the world that
a hot bath wouldn't help, just a little bit.
—*Susan Glasee*

HYGIENIC

If you go long enough without a bath,
even the fleas will leave you alone.
—*Ernie Pyle*

Sometimes "What the hell?" is the best answer to the question.

—Unknown

IMPULSIVE

Reason only controls us after emotion and
impulse have lost their impetus.

—Carlton Simon

The perfection of a life with a dog, like the perfection of an autumn, is disturbing because you know, even as it begins, that it must end. Time bestows the gift and steals it in the process.

—*George Bird Evans*

INEVITABILITY

A good dog never dies. He always stays. He walks beside you on crisp autumn days when frost is on the fields and winter's drawing near, his head is within our hand in his old way.

—*Mary Carolyn Davies*

I am neither especially clever nor especially gifted, only very, very curious

—*Albert Einstein*

INQUISITIVE

The one real object of education is to be in the condition of continually asking questions.

—*Bishop Mandell Creighton*

Boredom is an emptiness filled with insistence.

—*Leo Stein*

INSISTENT

You sometimes cannot ask to have your own
way, instead you must insist on it.

—*Unknown*

In order to make us covet a thing, it is only necessary to make the thing difficult to obtain.

—*Mark Twain*

JEALOUSY

Envy is the art of counting the other fellow's blessings instead of your own.

—*Harold Coffin*

Don't ask me to leave you and turn back. I will
go where you go and live where you live.

—*the Bible*

LOYALTY

A dog is the only thing on earth that loves
you more than he loves himself.

—*Josh Billings*

You have to expect things of yourself before you can do them.

—*Michael Jordan*

MOTIVATED

Believe in yourself! Have faith in your abilities! Without
a humble but reasonable confidence in your own
powers you cannot be successful or happy.

—*Norman Vincent Peale*

A day without a nap is like
a cupcake without frosting.
—*Terri Guillemets*

NAP TIME

I count it as a certainty that
in paradise, everyone naps.
—*Tom Hodgkinson*

Whenever there is authority, there is a
natural inclination to disobedience.
—*Thomas C. Haliburton*

NAUGHTY

It's no use growing older if you only learn
new ways of misbehaving yourself.
—*Hector Hugh Munro*

True nobility is exempt from fear.

—*Marcus Tullius Cicero*

NOBLE

Grave eyes, grave bearing, dignity of kings; The gentleness and trust as of a child; The flawless poise that veils old savage things. But half-remembered from the vanished wild.

—*C.T. Davis*

Teachability and trust always
leads to total obedience.

—*Ed Townsend*

OBEDIENCE

It is for each of us freely to choose
whom we shall serve, and find in
that obedience our freedom.

—*Mary Richards*

If your dog doesn't like someone, you probably shouldn't either.

—*Unknown*

OBSERVANT

If you think dogs can't count, try putting three biscuits in
your pocket and then giving Fido only two of them.

—*Phil Pastoret*

Realize that ultimate success comes from opportunistic,
bold move which, by definition, cannot be planned.

—*Ross Johnson*

OPPORTUNISTIC

Nothing is so often irretrievably missed as a daily opportunity.

—*Mari von Ebner-Eschenbach*

The bond with a true dog is as lasting as
the ties of this earth will ever be.
—*Konrad Lorenz*

PARTNERS

He is your friend, your partner, your defender, your dog.
You are his life, his love, his leader. He will be yours,
faithful and true, to the last beat of his heart.
You owe it to him to be worthy of such devotion.
—*Unknown*

Boredom is the feeling that everything is a waste of time; serenity, that nothing is.

—*Thomas S. Szasz*

PEACE

Each one has to find his peace from within. And peace to be real must be unaffected by outside circumstances.

—*Mahatma Gandi*

Never give up. Never give up, never, never, never, never.
—*Winston Churchill*

PERSISTENT

Perseverance and persistence in spite of all obstacles: It is this,
that in all things distinguishes the strong soul from the weak.
—*Thomas Carlyle*

Live and work but do not forget to play,
to have fun in life and really enjoy it.
—*Eileen Caddy*

PLAYFUL

We are never more fully alive, more completely
ourselves, or more deeply engrossed in
anything than when we are playing.
—*Charles Schaefer*

Sometimes questions are more important than the answers.

—*Nancy Willard*

QUESTIONING

Learn from yesterday, live for today, hope for tomorrow. The important thing is not to stop questioning.

—*Albert Einstein*

There is no sincerer love
than the love of food.

—*George Bernard Shaw*

RAVENOUS

One of the very nicest things about life is the
way we must regularly stop whatever it is we
are doing and devote our attention to eating.

—*Luciano Pavarotti*

Repentance is not so much remorse for what we
have done as the fear of the consequences.

—*Francois de la Rochefoucauld*

REPENTANT

Don't be angry with me for long, and don't lock
me up as punishment. You have your work,
entertainment and friends. I only have you.

—*Unknown*

Be content with what you have, rejoice in the way things are. When you realize there is nothing lacking, the whole world belongs to you.

—*Lao Tzu*

SIMPLICITY

They do not for all their marvelous instincts appear to know about death. Being such wonderfully uncomplicated beings, they need us to do their worrying.

—*George Bird Evans*

When you come to the end of your rope, tie a knot and hang on.

—*Franklin D. Roosevelt*

STUBBORNNESS

Stubbornly persist, and you will find that the limits of your stubbornness go well beyond the stubbornness of your limits.

—*Robert Brault*

The trouble with resisting temptation is
that it may never come your way again.

—*Korman's Law*

TEMPTATION

There is a charm about the forbidden that
makes it unspeakably desirable.

—*Mark Twain*

Forbearance is the root of quietness and assurance forever.
—*Ieyasu Tokugawa*

TOLERANT

When you find peace within yourself,
you can live at peace with others.
—*Unknown*

I didn't know it was impossible when I did it.

—*Unknown*

UNCANNY

The world is divided into two classes, those who believe
the incredible and those who do the improbable.

—*Oscar Wilde*

One breed, three colors, and
countless personalities.
—*Steve Smith, from* Just Labs

VARIETY

Variety's the very spice of life,
that gives it all its flavor.
—*William Cowper*

Life is one grand, sweet song, so start the music.

—*Ronald Reagan*

VOCAL

If you're quiet, you're not living. You've got to be noisy, colorful and lively.

—*Mel Brooks*

The most affectionate creature in the world is a wet dog.

—*Ambrose Bierce*

WATERPROOFED

To do anything truly worth doing, I must not stand back shivering and thinking of the cold and danger, but jump in with gusto and scramble through as well as I can.

—*Og Mandino*

How old would you be if you didn't know how old you are?

—*Satchel Paige*

YOUTHFUL

We don't stop playing because we grow old; we
grow old because we stop playing.

—*George Bernard Shaw*

Today is life—the only life you are sure of. Make the most of today. Let the winds of enthusiasm sweep through you.

–Dale Carnegie

ZEST

Dance as though no one is watching you; love as though you have never been hurt before, sing as though no one can hear you, live as though heaven is on earth.

—Alfred Souza